Fun Run

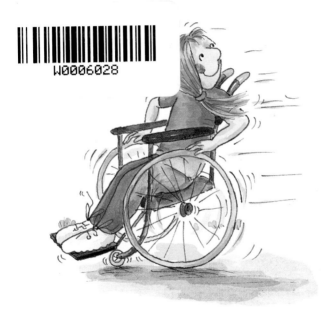

Written by Barrie Wade
Illustrated by Merida Woodford

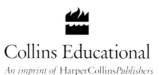

Collins Educational
An imprint of HarperCollins*Publishers*

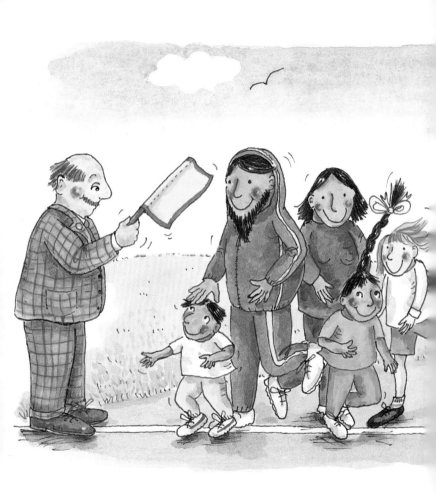

Off we go.

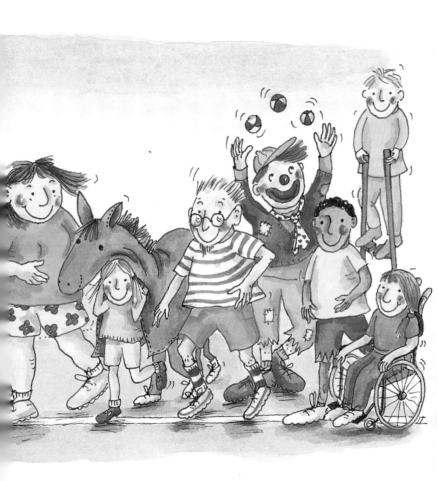

Don't be slow.

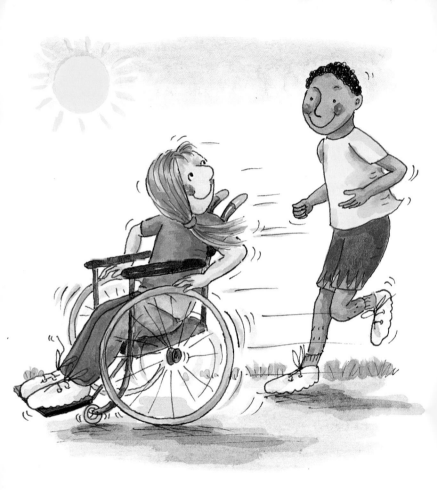

She's fast.

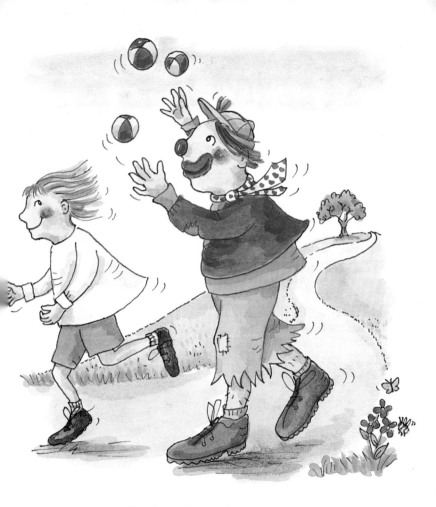

He's last.

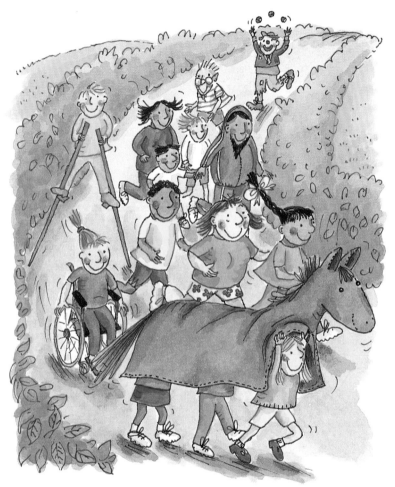

Round the bend.

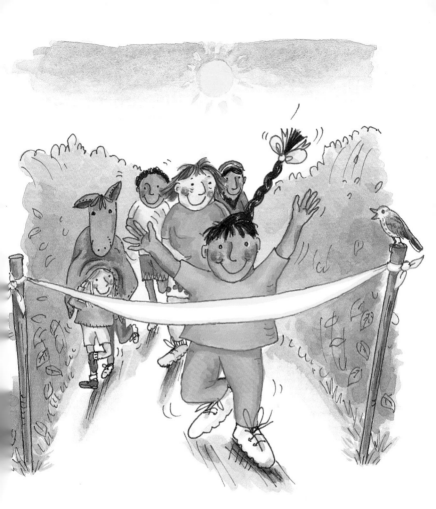

The end.

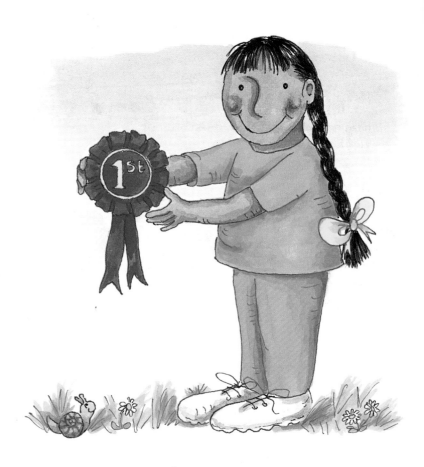

I won the fun run!